The Highwayman's Wife

The Highwayman's Wife

Poems

Lynnell Edwards

RED HEN PRESS | *Los Angeles, California*

The Higwayman's Wife
Copyright © 2007 by Lynnell Edwards

Book design by Mark E. Cull

Cover photograph from the "California Flea Markets"Series, Untitled 50
1977 © Joel D. Levinson

ISBN: 978-1-59709-075-9
Library of Congress Catalog Card Number: 2007920076

The City of Los Angeles Department of Cultural Affairs, Los Angeles County Arts
Commission and National Endowment for the Arts partially support Red Hen Press.

Published by Red Hen Press

JUL 0 8 2011

Acknowledgements

The following have appeared or are forthcoming:

Dogwood: *"The Highwayman's Wife"*; *Dos Passos Review*: *"Aubade, Kentucky Son"*; *Eclipse*: *"Driving Your Car"*; *Fugue*: *"Planting Dahlias With A Pick-Ax"*; *The Heartland Review*: *"Children, Sex"*; *Louisville Review*: *"Aubade, November"*; *New Millenium Writings*: *"The Last Long Days of Seventh Grade"*; *Pleiades*: *"All I Know About Love"*; *Smartish Pace*: *"For You, October's Boy," "Me, the Wife: Versions of Medusa"*; *Southern Poetry Review*: *"No Bigger Than A Minute"*; *Poems & Plays*: *"Campari and Soda," "PGA Punch," "Garnish," "Children Will Drive You," "What the Dead Think"*; *Sow's Ear Poetry Review*: *"I Gave My Love a Cell Phone"*; *Valparaiso Poetry Review*: *"The Offices of Flowers"*; *Poetry International*: *"Love, Helen," "Unraveling," "Trophy"*; *Riven*: *"And Matthew Brady Photographing It All"*.

Thanks to Jim Grabill for comments on an early version of the manuscript and to Gaylord Brewer for his insights. Thanks also to Virgil Suarez for his words of enthusiasm and to Cecilia Woloch for her generous reading and endorsement of the work, and to Wes, always.

Contents

prelude
Sonnet for the Highwayman   13

I. *leave no trace*
Cold As   17
Last Call: Campari and Soda   19
Suite for Wives
    I.   Me, The Wife: Versions of Medusa   20
    II.   Love, Helen   22
    III. Juno, Her Rival   24
    IV. Unraveling   26
    V.   Trophy   28
Last Call: Manhattan   30
Vocations of the Sleepless   31
Walking With the Hounds   32
What the Dead Think   34
The Offices of Flowers   35
Anniversary   36
Last Call: PGA Punch   37
California Redemption Value   38
Leave No Trace   40
Aubade, November   41
Bargain, Spent   42
Last Call: Old Fashioned   44
Loco Ceviche   45
Twister Takes Up Teen; Lives To Tell   46
Deadheading   48
And Matthew Brady Photographing It All   49
Campaign Promise   50
Last Call: Mint Julep   51
Garnish   52

II. *enter the highwayman*

Go   55

How It's Done   56

Weapons, The Road   57

The Problem of Debt   58

Wench (Lament for the Innkeep's Daughter)   59

The Problem of Roommates   60

Younger Brother Abroad   61

The Vicar's Dilemma   62

The Highwayman's Wife   63

The Moon, Spurned   64

Garrison Guns   65

III. *local concerns*

The Last Long Days of Seventh Grade   69

Spelling Test   71

Gardener's Almanac   72

In My New Expanded Life   73

No Regrets   74

Aubade, Kentucky Son   75

Alabama Interlude

    I.   The Baby Plays Monopoly   76

    II. Lakebottom   78

    III. Damp   79

Further Affections   80

Vacation Rental   81

All I Know About Love   82

Sidelined, Coach   84

Driving Your Car   86

Planting Dahlias With A Pick-Ax   88

For You, October's Boy   89

I Gave My Love A Cell Phone;
    or, Technology Won't Help You Now   90
Children, Sex   91
Children Will Drive You   92
No Bigger Than A Minute   94
Advice to the Poet   95
The November Shakes   96
On Presuming Mr. James Caan Would Not,
    Under Any Circumstances, Pretzel   98
Snow Day   99

prelude

I

leave no trace

Cold As

Whose almanacks thumbd pages swarm
Wi frost and snow and many a storm
And wisdom gossipd from the stars
Of polities and bloody wars
He shakes his head and still proceeds
Neer doubting once of what he reads
All wonders are wi faith supplyd

　　　　　　　　—John Clare, "January"
　　　　　　　　The Shepherd's Calendar

It is cold this morning, cold as
ice cream with the Eskimos, cold
as a witch's, cold as the comfort
of the brute alarm that pulled you
into this darkness. And try
as you might to read the signs
of opaque winter: snow drift balanced
on a mounded shrub; black bird
lofted in the low-vaulted sky; maze
of bare branches, their map of bloom
and struggle; axis of ice adhered
to the limestone pass, its cold flow
halted in portent chunks;
still the day reveals nothing distinct
from days past, no clue
to the new year, how it will unfold
loosed from this cold morning, cold
as a sunken stone, cold as blue blazes.

But could you divine whether
now frozen fields would exceed
or fail their demanded yield; whether
tight-lipped accounts would compound,
seed, or disappear; whether travel, study,
spirit flayed into its raw, component parts
(you'll be *better* this year, more faithful
in your prayers), would bring you
fat to harvest, smacking your lips
with the sweet wine of success, would you
take your bootless, bare-chested brag
into this cold? (Cold as that last day
in hell, cold as the blood of the dead.)
Such cold perversion of fortune would set
your compass spinning, leave you cold-
cocked, iced. So mute January
gives you only this cold offering:
tinny clank of silver its only gift,
white slate blank for your rough mark.

Last Call: Campari and Soda

Make it like the Italy you've always
imagined. Think: *piazzo.* Think: *ciao
bella.* Think: garnet alchemy
of root and herb and time. Ignore
the cocktail crowd, hot and rumpled;
ignore the hangers-on beginning
to stagger and slur; ignore the jerk
in the stained tie who wants to know:
What's the red stuff sweetie?
Think: tiled verandas, slim linen suits.
Ignore the bitterness at your lips; say:
Trade secrets. Bene. Exquisite.

Suite for Wives

I. Me, The Wife: Versions of Medusa

One day it will come to this:

Me, in the cave
of our kitchen,
flexing and wet,
music so loud
the walls throb, me
slicing meat
with the biggest knife
you've ever seen,
for a devil stew
you're afraid to eat,
certain I've chopped up
the children or worse. Or

me, upstairs, in our dark
bedroom, eyes
drifting and mystic,
candle and incense smoke
throat-choking thick, me
stammering prophecy
from the great omphalos
of our bed: *every way*
in is also a way out.
Evidence of ropes, every
nail a different color. Or

me, instead, outside
ground down into the brown
earth of our garden,
chanting for rain and shaking
the root bone of a white rose,
my face bruised
and streaked, my hair
clotted with weeds.

And when it does,
get the mirror,
the reflective shield,
oh my clever Perseus,
even the flat side
of your shining sword.
But do not look upon this;
you will not live to tell.

II. Love, Helen

All Greece hates
the still eyes in the white face,
the luster as of olives
where she stands,
and the white hands.
                      —*H.D.*, "Helen"

A thousand fucking ships
to recover my sweet ass?
What fools. And that's not
the half of it. Listen, bitch:
I wanted out. Out
of that palace house, prison
of Spartan glint and despair;
out from under the sexless
slump of the old man,
his stale breath, palsied grip;
out from the clutches
of the brats we begot, immortals'
burden to issue heirs. Out
of it all, sister. So when
that fine shepherd showed
his sweet face, the swan
in me lifted to meet his mouth,
wild bird heart swollen
like a sail in the Aegean breeze,
his hands on the arc
of my cygnet neck, his hands
sculpting the hollow of my waist,
now winged love soaring

across the waves, the wine-dark
flush of desire unconstrained,
now my marble silence
tightening as a noose
around Troy's breath. And you
want to know why and how
much and when.

I say: take your goddamn thousand ships,
rattling songs of arms and the man,
clarion gifts that seethe revenge,
but know this: when the long battle
years wage on and you wait
for your man while age bends
your brittle frame, spots
your once-milky skin, thins
your fertile hair where he buried
his tears, released his joy,
know this: I am beautiful
still; your men, all dead.

III. Juno, Her Rival

But the vengeance of Juno was not yet satiated. She sent a gadfly to
torment Io, who fled over the whole world from its pursuit.
                                        —Bullfinch's Mythology

I know your dreams, lithe
Io, the dangerous
ones. Domestic, complete,
I know how you imagine
he clothes, feeds you,
how you would perch, flushed,
on the counter in my kitchen
wearing his white shirt,
clever in the crook
of your hooked arms,
bent knees. You watch him
crush garlic with oil,
take his offering, the crust
from his fingertips,
the wine to your lips, meat
from the shining blade.

You would recline
in the swing on the wide,
planked porch, wearing
his work boots, happy
in the rock and sway,
arms extended as he brings
dahlias, roses, asters, lilies
chopped from my garden. Or

most subtle treachery
of all, you are faint
from heat or storm of fever
and to soothe he fashions
schoolboy's verses: how
dear the blush and fumble
when he reads the ink-fresh lines.

But to hide this
deception, he must
bloat the soft hollows
of hip and thigh
where he rests his head,
lays his soft hands,
sprout you horns
at crazed angles from
a head that lolls
on a loose and fleshy neck.
And you will curse
the short rope of tail,
knotted with filth and hair

that swats a black gnat
I have sent to bite
your patched and mange-
scarred flank, spur you
eternally displaced, damned
in your animal stagger to madness.

IV. Unraveling

Now all these lies he made appear so truthful,
she wept as she sat listening.
          —The Odyssey, Book XIX

I get the reports, hear
the news, see
the e-mail distributions:
whirlpool   rock   financial ruin
your triumph or
defeat, how your men
were lost, transformed
utterly, your silence
from the island.

I have received
the gifts over
these long years:
the lacquered box,
wedding cup,
tortoise comb and mirror,
each catalogued by
its occasion missed.

And I have made marks
on the wall for the boy,
notched the door frame
for each year, driven
the miles to school and sport,
and now by his embrace
I feel him taller, broader
than I remember you.

These men that line
the halls will not wait,
their plans, their contests
more elaborate each day.
They ask what I make:
travel cloak or cape, blanket,
subtle tapestry. But nothing

in my smile betrays
the end: a net
my love, for your return
and soon.

V. Trophy

I have done with tears. I will endure my death.
　　　　　　　—Cassandra. from Agamemnon,
　　　　　　　Aeschylus' *Oresteia*

Agamemnon, baby, hot
from acquisition, trade,
splendid astride your plunder,
speed me across
the wine-dark lake
in your terrible vessel.
Gilt me as you will:
I am your morning glory, daylily,
bikini-clad figurehead
wedged in the thrust
of a cigarette-sleek bow.
Burden my limbs
with stones the color
of bone and blood.
Buy me a ring
that will cut and shine.
Gun us past the deep channel,
the sheer cliff, the lesser
men in their lesser crafts.
Shred the wake
into white madness,
cutting spray. Agamemnon,
sweetheart, outrace the dark horizon,
thunderheads gnarled
with the surging storm.
Carry me heaving and damp
to your marble halls.

So what you do not hear
my cry above the whine
and saw of horsepower,
the smack of wave against
the hull? So what if
the clattering boast
of other men's gold
shutters the arc of my wail?
So you do not know
the brutal truth of my possession—
the flash of cloaked knife,
the end in nets and slaughter—
the ride, Agamemnon
darling, wasn't it a ride?

Last Call: Manhattan

Make it mother-in-law sweet,
the best whiskey you can find
muddled with sugar at the bottom
of a squat crystal goblet.
And don't stint on the fruit, the speared
orange lemon cherry thrust through
cracked ice, the bitters swirling
at the base like oil,
the evening's best dressed high,
sweating in a bright paper napkin.

Vocations of the Sleepless

One like a Chinese philosopher stands
slack before the yawning refrigerator,

baptized in cold light. Another
a bookie, figures odds against

dawn, his pay-off decreasing
with each crawling minute.

The banker re-finances; receipts
unfurl before his blinking eyes.

The alcoholic spasms, drummed up
from black stupor. Frantic parents

stumble to cribs, desperate lovers
pace by the phone. The doubt,

the debt, the granite-sized guilt;
the apocalypse of lights left on,

appliances running, numbers rounded up,
I need to call that guy back.

What could come of our evening pleas?
Now I lay me down to sleep.

The bargain is struck; slippery night comes;
the other cheek turns to the slap of day:

I pray the Lord my soul to take.

Walking With the Hounds

The foddering boy forgets his song
And silent goes wi' folded arms
And croodling shepherds bend along
Crouching to the whizzing storms

—*John Clare*, "February"
The Shepherd's Calendar

My father and I are walking through rough fields
that rattle and sigh when we pass through rows that were
corn, late squash, hay now bent and soured
for months. A burden of earth adheres to our soles,
dampens our cuffs. It is late, we think; the sky
is grey, the white sun low. For hours we
have walked with the group, trailing the dogs from yelp
to frantic yelp as they scent and chase their prey.
Now they swarm our feet, a hive of teeth
and tails, straining muzzles. They lead us to
a ruined barn, grey-planked, sagging, tin-roof
fallen in, a bale of wire unspooling
at one corner, a broken-toothed mower
yawning in the surrounding yard. Inside,
we know, the hare races, wild and bright
with instinct, dumb to our sport. But we have
no guns, no horses, no desire for trophies
flayed and tallied, so we call the pups'
retreat, encourage with a shout and stick
a homeward point, a sinkhole of rock and bramble
near the kennel. My father and I fall
behind, consider the burden to plow these February
fields, the shoulder and the thigh of it
still required, even with machine
and hired help, to unleash Demeter's
wild heart from winter grief, release

the singing green, lush abundant bloom.
And I see him there alone, walking
with the hounds from equinox to
equinox, wandering without light
in sorrow's dry and frozen furrow.

What the Dead Think

Not of the family farm, plowed under
or preserved, its acres torn among
a storm of siblings; not of the second
spouse, cruel and beautiful wearing
their jewelry, reading their books;
not of the secret lover taken in youth,
letters discovered in a closeted box;
not of their bodies or hair, the frantic shuffle
to adorn and disguise. But of that black
plinth before them always: push it forward
or go around? Scratch its glassy surface
for a seam or shatter it with a fist? How
to remember thinking, choice, from this urging
swirl of amnesia, that there is an order
to remembering, a reason to take
those first infant breaths toward return.

The Offices of Flowers

The tulips left late
in the vase
have this morning surrendered
dry petals
to the table top.

Stalks gone slick
and soft, I lift
the bunch, bleeding
water, leaf,
carry it out
through the house,
find a place
to rest the limpid stems.

Again I have required
too much from
the offices of flowers:
that they hold their pose;
open, close another week;
flash their campaign of color, seed;
scent and bloom
the rest of my life.

Anniversary

A maid at night by treacherous love decoyd
Was in that shrieking wood years past destroyd
She went twas said to meet the waiting swain
And home and friends ne'er saw her face again
                              —*John Clare*, "March"
                              The Shepherd's Calendar

Back to the scene of the crime, then. Back to the scene
of violence, spent evidence of harvest, the mass
of matted leaves, stems hunched in piles, unidentified.
In this last hour of light, you survey the garden
now a grave of thistle, burr; best intentions of vine

and stalk gone to rot. Winter pries at your collar, hem.
Hands jammed in pockets you consider how to raise the dead,
cheat frost, damage mend. Guilty man, you'll confess
the old infractions: insect, drought, neglect, and mark
this anniversary with covenant renewed and green,

until she rises from the rotted furrows, faint in till tracks
rough with clotted clay. While at the slashed edge of the earth
the low blooms do all cry, their flower mouths a stain:
my god, but did you love her; didn't she suffer enough.

Last Call: PGA Punch

Make it in thirty-two gallon plastic
garbage cans: half pure grain,
half whatever flavor drink-aide
best matches the party's theme:
orange at Halloween; green at Christmas;
red on St. Valentine's Day when she
walks into the basement at the house
where you've been pledging all night,
staggers to the bar, hair in her face,
Miss Mascara in his lettered shirt, says she
never has had to pay for a drink at this house,
takes a ladleful of your lover's brew,
brimming, at exactly the price she deserves.

California Redemption Value

When the retirees next to me on the plane
say I must be native because I'm so tan,
and I get a free upgrade on my rental car

without asking, and when the 405 is clear
all the way south, but for the guy on the cell
in the convertible one lane away who smiles

and winks and then roars ahead,
a shimmering show of force, I'll take it.
And doesn't the sun light my face

at the beach café, and isn't that an actor
at the near table talking to his agent
because, why not? This is California

where the curl of each blue wave
breaks in laced symmetry, and the sky
is a lapis slate clear to Catalina.

And shopping in the hip district
always yields impossible bargains,
and dinner at the rock star's house suggests

an impromptu acoustic session, specially
recorded in house, and sleeping
in a strange bed still feels like home.

And I know salvation takes more
than traveling to another state,
that the equation for redemption is more

complex than the exchange of evergreen gloom
for stalked and swaying palms, but I would
give my last nickel for it this morning,

and what it all comes down to:
a breakfast table set for two women,
heads together, their eyes, mouths

in confidence; their purchases
and affairs, offspring and house,
plans to take over the world.

Leave No Trace

Refill the drained bottle;
make the bed.
Pack everything out;
settle accounts.
Cover tracks, and
walk in the surf,
each footprint reclaimed
by a breaking wave.

Do not stir the dust.
Do not turn the stones.
Do not blow spark into flame,
but be like

the stars' cold light
that spills no shadow;
or the high drifting clouds
stitched to the horizon;
or the slim branch falling
into the forest pool,
its widening geometry
sighing against the shore.

Aubade, November

Winter gets in
to the chimney first,
rain like rivets
on tin that wakes
my body's husk,
aching and clenched
against the cold.

The wind fits
its knife edge
to the sills,
hisses in, troubles
the drapes, slicks the glass
with its cracked chill.

And you wake too,
bent arm wrapping
my waist, splayed hand
finding a knob of hip,
a furrow of rib,
some aftermath to glean,

some not yet gathered bloom.

Bargain, Spent

What I've become
Troubles me even if I shut my eyes.

—*Randall Jarrell*, "Next Day"

Saturday morning at the supermarket and the old men
wheel their baskets past one another, acknowledge
the mutual plight with a subtle nod. Billed caps perched
on stubbled pates, khaki pants sagging at the rear,
shirt pockets stuffed with pens, glasses, small notepads,
they forage in the past-date meat bin, at the wall
of canned vegetables *(so many kinds of tomatoes these days);*
troll the manager's specials aisle for post-season deals:
chocolate hearts, flag-stamped napkins, pumpkin plates.
In one fist he clutches a list: *get these things.*
And spilling from a hip pocket coupons
clipped from the Friday circular: two-for-one
English muffins; twenty-four count toilet paper
three dollars off with purchase of cleaner;
potatoes, ten pounds for two dollars; and most
magnificent: green peppers five for a dollar.
He counts out ten, surveys each for its color, shape,
then places them in a sack, stashes it snug.
Satisfied, he nudges his cart into line behind
a mother and child; she is bleary, stained, beautiful
lifting bread and milk and butter onto the conveyor.
He smiles, remembers his grandson about the same age,
thinks to comment on the their early start, but she
eyes his absurd bounty, shifts the infant, looks away.
What was it his friend said on retirement?
Find a hobby? Travel? Take up golf? No. Don't
go to the barber and the bank on the same day,
watch your hands as they go spotted, soft.
Home, his wife wants to know what to do

42

with ten green peppers: *They'll rot.*
What kind of bargain is it then?
And he doesn't know. Or once knew, then forgot.

Last Call: Old Fashioned

Make it in a gallon pickle jar,
round and smooth as a fat man's gut.
Use Pop's family recipe, passed
down from generation upon generation,
the rinds of boiled lemons, suspended
in a brew of whisky and sugar and bitters.
Find a cool, dark place to let your secret
sit two weeks, at least. Then bring it out
for the holidays, your sweet brown baby,
sparkling in the swirl of the season.

Loco Ceviche

Not even a goddamn banana since
dry toast on the boat at eight bells
and now already past one. Our guts
rumble, heads float and nod like buoys,
clanging with hunger's reptile insistence.
So when the wind kicks up
on the island's north side,
we retreat to the nearest fish shack,
settle into plastic chairs and watch
the ferries scramble like rats
across the curdled slough.
We catch the boy hustling past,
order *mixte grande*, splash
the platter with habaneros, lime,
scoop the wicked fix onto crackers,
while the crooner tunes up,
sets his drum machine throbbing
over the American track.
We gulp short glasses
of iced wine and *cerveza*,
which sounds like *ceviche*
to my gringo ears, like singing
lisped across hot tin, bright
sting of green and white,
the swirl and blur it will all become.

Twister Takes Up Teen; Lives to Tell

Thou lovley april fare thee well
Thou early child of spring
Tho born where storms too often dwell
Thy parents news to bring

—John Clare, "April"
The Shepherd's Calendar

Just after nine and the boy already dead
asleep. Exhausted from a turkey shoot at dawn,
he falls into sleep mute and deep as roots in dirt.
Out back, his parents clean up the barbecue,
first warm night since the time change, see off
the neighbors down the way, their backs turned
to darkness hunched on the horizon. Inside,
quiet. The last dim light becoming strange,
then, *we heard a kind of roaring, like*
the air conditioner come on, and *all*
of a sudden-like, hail sharp as buckshot
against the shutters, fingers of trees
clawing at the windows, then *the door*
just blowed off its hinges, sails
into the front room like a sled down
the winter slope. They remember the boy,
and scramble through the darkness, pull
against the suck of pressure: all gone.
Walls, roof, bed – second story clean
as a cleared field. Instinct sends them
back down the stairs to a rattle and bang
at the back porch and *Mercy!* There he
stands, needing nineteen stitches
and a wet rag, but alright. *I didn't know*
which way was up nor down, he will
later tell reporters. He can't recall

being plucked from his bed, tumbled
like a rock over the creek bottom,
his arms, legs, wild vines searching
like the live pupil in a dark eye,
tossed out into a country strange as OZ:
cars balanced in the narrow forks
of trees; a single straw driven through
a plank of fence; a man's tool shed intact,
while the barn attached splintered. The boy's
own bed frame, mattress found three-hundred fifty
yards away, unscarred. *I don't know how long
I was in there,* the newspaper will record.
*I didn't know what was going to happen
to me.* It's storm season, son, April surge
of wind and bone. What did you expect?

Deadheading

Evident death already at the equinox:
the jonquil heads like the fists of old women,
tissue thin, withered, nodding in the sun;
tulip petals blown from their stems,
stamens bald, unashamed; the white poplars
blasted to tatters, littering the yard.

How this brown and crumpled flare of spring persists,
even as we beat back emerald lawns each weekend,
and the wisteria claws its way across the eaves.
The hardwoods rattle the ruffled sleeves on knotty arms,

and we scratch new wounds in the earth,
blanket infant shoots with bone and dirt,
mound and cover against certain frost, pray
an impossible lullaby of water, light, forgiveness.

And Matthew Brady Photographing It All

How those first photographs stun them
In New York, battlefields wrecked
With bodies bloated and still as fish, eyes white,
Screwed toward the preponderance of sky.
Every horizon low in the frame, every border
Bleeds to the edge. This the war that started
As a fray on a grassy hill, a few shots volleyed across
Calm water, a local action easily patched.
But now here it is, chromatic, huge, hanging
At eye level, piled against the warehouse walls.
The photos overfill the gallery, spill into the papers
Where mothers see their moon-faced boys for the first time
Among the dead, stacked and charred like timber,
Strewn like dolls against a sand embankment,
Bandaged and slumped across a cannon.
Now the lists of dead grow longer. Now the shutters
Click at will in the camps where Brady's men
Roam unchecked. Now the lens widens to embrace
The apocalypse of Shiloh, the terror of Antietam,
"The Hornet's Nest," "The Slaughter Pen,"
"The Harvest of Death," "The Devil's Den."
Just a little more light, just a little more speed
Now, and he will frame the shot, the fall
The ascendance into heaven that gives us
Something for our papers, something for our pain.

Campaign Promise

Which he at early morning leaves
The driving boy beside his team

—*John Clare*, "May"
The Shepherd's Calendar

Wide open the field, they said, wide open.
Anyone's race to lose – why not you? They said,
you're a good man, family head, friends you trust
from playground days, college bouts. You've seen
hardship, battle, come through unbent. And we need
good men to keep us straight. So name filed in winter,
you beat hard scandal, smear, betrayal from inside,
and came through worn to primary May, the open field
broken wide apart. Now every smile, firm handshake,
flat palm placed not too heavy, not too light
on every sturdy back plies the margin wide or slim.
Every name must be recalled at every baseball game,
each boy's hit, strong run, a cause for celebration.
Every portent clink of ice at every cocktail toast
must be divined; every dollar-raising thank you
after dinner must get reply. And final Sunday school
amen is now logged weekly to document repentance,
desire for sweet salvation. Now no man's job,
civic vision is insignificant; no mother's fear,
sweet dream too slight. There is no *no*.
These final May campaigns, you cheer
both sides, declare two winners, pay all bets.
The field is set, contest nearly ended
but for the final race across the open field.
And you imagine horses, men, brute persistence,
relentless whip and spur to best the finish line.

Last Call: Mint Julep

Make it despite impossible odds,
trifecta of sugar, sweet mint,
bourbon tipped over ice,
sipped slow. Then wait
for the rush and burn, that horse
no one suspected, that six furlong finish,
your goddamn luck that will never run out.

Garnish

As desired. Though not essential,
the wedge of lime or orange,
slick cherry, bald olive or onion
for some is the very substance
of the style, perched on the rim,
speared through the ice,
or sunk and lolling
in the bottom of the glass.

II

enter the highwayman

Go

Three days ago he'd packed his case, shined
his boots and bit, but could not lift the latch.
He's not a superstitious man, but wheeling winds
and portent birds, salt spilled, ashes
arrayed in troubling drifts suggested finer
times to go. So when the night arrives,
wood and larder stocked, wife resigned
and sighing by her lonesome stove, neighbor
bribed to keep the whiskey under lock,
he hears the rafters and the hinges hissing *go*
No road is calling, no lover taunting, no
unmade fortune pulls him from his house
to abandon favorite chair, faithful hound,
just the shutters and the windows mouthing *go*

How It's Done

When drunkards stagger from the lighted inn,
or husbands travel to town, helpless, burdened
with a foundered hog, a ragged goat,
ambush is the surest. Brutish, quick, the novice
way to thieve, it guarantees a modest
haul: some gold, a gun, a woolen cloak.
A knifepoint and a level stare is all you need.
Call it highway tax, or ferry toll: your due receipt.
But for the wayward coach the expert guile
is to ride along beside, affect a lover's smile,
offer help, safe passageway and then assassinate
the driver. Unloose and whip the beasts,
snap the brittle limb of life they clutch and shake,
hoping something that falls from it you'll take.

Weapons, the Road

Pistols, derringers, daggers, ropes, no matter
what you pack you're not prepared. Disaster
happens quick from lack of feed as powder,
your beast no more certain than the weather:
rain that ruins roads, wind that punishes speed,
heat and sun that kick up dust, make travelers recede
into the quavering, liquid sky. There is no way to gauge
how much water, bread, or gold a fortnight takes.
The necessity of bribes for territories broached,
a fretting lover, unpaid bill, all of these you know
will make a good man stumble, scramble to employ
some compensatory measure, forage for reserves,
a safer route, alibis, whiskey for his nerves,
and a superstitious man, mere bad luck will destroy.

The Problem of Debt

The young man's way to settle gaming debts
no longer wears. Whiskey, pistols, what you get
dependent on a knife point jammed between
finger, thumb, palms slapped flat first
on the money pot, steady eyes, tight smile,
the girl behind the bar, her nod, her sign to hold
or fold tendered every night. Now no matter how mean
your grasp on gold, it clatters from your hand:
the farrier, wheelwright, blacksmith, coachman,
they'll be there on your return, rattling receipts,
the black X marking the accounts you owe,
calling you into the wretched, howling cold,
reminding you of the promise that you made,
the kind of girl she was, what she offered to pay.

Wench
(*Lament for the Innkeep's Daughter*)

The word comes out hard, hissed from their jaws: *wench.*
The tool, the means, the object that she is, and the less
she says the better on these apocalyptic nights when
massed like snakes, weapons close, the highwaymen
coil and slide about his inn, call for beer, the *wench*
to bring it straightaway. And when she smiles, again
the shock of laughter crashes through the room, their bets
slapped flat under overturned tankards. He wishes then
a different story for his daughter than barkeep for these men.
A snug stone house, roses on the wall, gentle beasts – a hen
for laying, sheep for milk, a fat sow and her litter penned,
and all along the back, lavender and sage, a square garden
where her mother stands working, smiling there again,
and calls to him, laughing, bitter, bright, the *wench.*

The Problem of Roommates

Not least of all, is that they snore.
And when a man is hollow with fatigue, what more
does he want than dreamless, deadening sleep?
And further, while you rest, they steal,
smuggle small goods from your leather pack,
unnoticed until later when you go back
for the bread, last drink of brandy, the book
of accounts, you find the knave has gone. The crook
has made his bed, paid his bill, left no
forward post; the inkeep just shrugs, says *So?*
Your loss. And it is. Again, another night
you meant to trust a fellow thief, and instead
of honor, found absence and deception, cold regret,
portent clouds, a rush of swallows, the story of your life.

Younger Brother Abroad

Brother, there are options here, fortunes to be got,
satchels to be cut, loose and fat, from belts
of boys. And merchanting (we'll call it that),
from ragged, unprotected coasts, we'll rob
them all. Let me make a passage here, a ship
I know, a man who owes. Let me take
you from that lonely road, that archaic
code of highway crime dependent on a bluff,
a guess at weapons, the speed of beasts, enough
darkness to escape. Prospect in this science
of the New World, this laboratory of slaughter
with savages for alibis, the yeoman's daughter
for our ransom. Abandon politics, the false proprietary
god that made you first, gave you the swinging light.

The Vicar's Dilemma

The way the money comes cannot be right,
in careless sackfuls, buckled chests,
scattered at the altar, beneath the feet of Christ.
It's all ill-gotten, blood ransom at very best,
seized at knifepoint, unholy bargaining for life:
mere amusement for the man. A whim, he guesses
that such ransom should be spilled to feed the poor,
clothe the wretched, suffer haven from the storm.
So why not fit the chapel too, with gold,
bright cruciforms, robes against the cold,
singeing incense, candles for the dead,
abundant wine, dark and rich, bread
sliced thick. This will force a man to pray,
compensate the souls he cannot save.

The Highwayman's Wife

Another moon past and again the persistent stain.
She wants a child. But no counted days,
or bed raised, tonic or tincture brings one.
He is always away, or at home so whiskied and loose,
distracted, rambling about some deal, how one day,
the next foreign port, and still her mind strays
to the fair brats, indistinct in the neighbor's lane,
the shouts of their game, the debris of their play
strewn across her sister's lawn. Bawling, squalling
day and night, she would fill this stone house
with toddling, spitting creatures; tie them in bunches
to her skirts, stack them at night in their little beds,
huddle them into her empty, empty arms,
and carry them into her marvelous, flower-filled yard.

The Moon, Spurned

Once she was as simple as a silver coin,
flat, round, bright and ripe for taking,
obvious, hanging in the sky, forsaken
by relentless day and its favorite righteous boy
who points and stares, leaves no man unmarked.
The best kind of lover: silent, whole, need
as smooth and hard as glass, that cools, recedes
when strategy demands that you discard
her for another kind of mistress, another way
through hazards and the traps, the clawing fray.
But riding on the silver road tonight,
your solitude betrays you. She throws her light
on your luckless run, indifference while you weep,
shows in trees and stones the outlines of defeat.

Garrison Guns

Half past noon the sun shafts through the shutters
of the rented room where, sleeping now, he stirs,
then winces in the light. Today he will return.
He reaches for his shirt, puts cold feet, one, another
on the floor. Thinks briefly of the road
toward home, the steeples, bridges, stones.
He stretches toward the ache of day,
counts receipts, begins to cipher loss and gain:
the money got against fatigue and loss,
while the regiment arms fire their shots
from far across the bay. He braces for the blast,
the punishing thuds a litany for the life he had:
the house he built, the wife he took, the brother
he loved, the righteous men and their garrison guns.

III

local concerns

The Last Long Days of Seventh Grade

The shepherd's leisure hours are over now
— John Clare, "June"
The Shepherd's Calendar

The last long days of seventh grade
unfurl glazed calm, windless,
breeding idleness in drifts
of prank and curse, and still you must
pace through, take successive
turns at locker, desk, wait
while summer's buzz and hum
blows aloft beyond the pavement lot.
And insult to injury, *The Old Man*
And the Sea, assigned this week
by a man who cannot imagine,
cannot fathom what it is
to be thirteen, cannot feel
how you burn to be released
to fields and lakes and evening streets.
How check marks, extra credit,
paper, book, and pen cannot
tell how life breaks across
the bow, and just as fast
washes away without you.
And still *The Old Man and the Sea*
pages on and on with it plotless song
of fish hooks and despair,
blistered hands, stooped and buckled
backs. *Metaphor!* The man in front
declaims. *Allegory! Write this down.*
There will be a test. So on and on
you slog, oars against the tide.
How this fragile boat of boyhood

has carried you so far I cannot say.
And how to navigate the latitudes,
I do not know. But there are horizons
plenty still, and dark shapes
swift beneath the cresting waves,
waiting on your line, testing
the pull on your bursting heart,
with the reel and spin of love.

for CWE IV

Spelling Test

Not the logic of sense, but of sound
that brings together *mountain* and *captain*
in a list, or *table* with *label*. Though no connection

exists between those flat surfaces, they are
mated this Friday for articulation. And all
the varieties of *there* and *hear* and *your*

without distinction except when used
in a sentence, please. Each word practiced
all week, the letters revealed in their singular

glory. Like the combination to a lock,
the letters tumble onto the page, a separate
line for each one, please, and no looking

at your neighbor's paper. Eyes ahead,
not drifting to the rain and the playground
and the puddles under the swings, slowly filling.

Gardener's Almanac

Under my averted eye,
even houseplants die.
Fern and ficus, spider, jade,
the unkillable wilt
from too much, not enough,
tiny mites, dust.
Window boxes
flame and fall for all
to see my shame.
Bulbs plunged late
in cold November earth
freeze or rot.
By June weeds choke
the vegetable project.
The pledge
to prune and stake,
pinch early blooms,
nurture, cultivate,
I break, and when
I do collect
the pitiful, persistent,
harvest it grows soft
and dark in the basket.
I will turn it all
under in the fall.
An afternoon of chopping,
spading until
the whole disaster –
tall, stalked, ragged, thin –
is buried; my satisfaction
tamping down the dirt,
raking smooth the plot.

In My New Expanded Life

There is room for all things: family, big house, career,
committed friendships, recreational sports, and unaccounted
others: exquisite, sweet, and dark. I am domestic

and fabulous, play the piano well this time,
have a newly toned body and a limber mind
that wraps itself around difficult concepts,

like string theory and God, foreign languages,
recipes that require you grind your own spices.
I possess sexual cleverness, intensity that would leave

a lover breathless, the aching imprint of my touch
singeing his skin for days, and still I can
comfort small children, stop their tears

with the trick of a coin, the magic of origami.
In this new expanded life, my heart does not
break. No longer a brittle clockworks destroyed

with each anachronistic sweep, this improved
organic ticker blooms and swells like a marvelous
sun, firing my soul to enhanced understandings

of love, world peace, and harmony
among the beasts. And I find a way
to walk outside when it looks like rain,

name what it is I really want, consider
its impossible heft in my open palm,
stand up straight in the sparking storm.

No Regrets

Rogue coastal thoughts unfurl
at my heart's headwaters,
a curdled stew of foam and weed,
swirling fantasy, drift:
Move to Europe! Take
a lover! Write a memoir
revealing how you fear
your mother, French-kissed
your brother! I could cast out
past the lighthouse
to more intriguing seas,
islands of complex ancient architecture,
flush with exotic birds,
perfumed and swollen fruit;
tack against the wind,
find rippling currents
to carry me through
unmarked furrows
of deep mazarine.
But with each receding tide
I hear the low tumble of boulders:
injury, shame grinding
at the shore. And I heave
my anchor toward that house,
the one I built on sand,
scramble with my shovel, dig.

Aubade, Kentucky Son

Fuck those Wildcats! you say because
this is the way we natives claim our blood.
You bring whiskey in a flask to the lecture,
cock one restless leg on the chair. You wander
aimless in the lobby; you've lost your lover,
your last joint. And if you make it out at all,
you hound-dog behind her, slack and awed.

The brief night hours are filled
with apologies, prayers, until graceless
and spent you are shooed from her room.
Of course it rains as you slouch to the street;
of course you are not prepared, and hiss
blunt curses at the jeering clouds:
Fuck those Wildcats. I know who you are.

Pounded out of the adolescent court
by bigger, faster boys. Lost in conversation
until your stammer and your anger
sound like honor and entitlement, that code
every boy before you suffers through
and every boy that you will father
must shoulder forward yet.

How hard to be from that country of lashing cold,
heaving heat. How hard to claim that laboring past,
that weak-chinned mountain line. And how hard
to stare down reconciliation when she touches
your stubbled cheek, sings her difficult
five-stringed song, and lifts her ragged, painted wings.
I would give it to you still.

Alabama Interlude

I. The Baby Plays Monopoly

Rain again on the second day, and the tattered
boxes are unshelved, hauled into
the center room for children to abuse.
They grab Monopoly, squabble for
the top hat, yacht, old shoe, train, initiate
the barter for Railroads, Park Place, *trade for
all the Reds.* Beyond the din adults relax and sigh
with newspapers, coffee, review the weather
signs, consider dinner plans, and someone
turns the baby loose, sets it babbling,
spitting into motion, spastic at their feet,
unseen now advancing toward the knot
of cousins tossing dice, their lullaby
of chatter, the flutter of their nimble hands.
And now the baby lurches huge beside
the game, its globe-like head bobbing, pushing
to their huddle. A blunt knee covers Jail;
one hand like a spatula flips a tiny,
gabled house. Another like Godzilla
smashes *GO*, and still the baby keeps
on coming. The brother lugs the baby sack-like
off the board, drops it squirming by
the chair. But the baby bleats and rights
itself, returns in greater force, scatters
Chance, flattens stacks of cash. A sister
tries confining it behind a desk,
distracts it with some plastic keys, but baby
will not relent, louder in its angry
squall, clever in its progress, until
the baby now sits flailing at the center

of the game, insisting in its right
to be the baby, the owner of all properties,
the arbiter of wealth, the last great family
tycoon making all the rules, chewing
up the fragile sibling contracts in its toothless
baby mouth, compounding all the debt
in its ferocious baby fists.

II. Lakebottom

Three days of rain and the water stirred
into muddy confluence, choked with debris,
grasses soaked from the banks, the surface
scummed and still, frothed air pockets
belched up from below, where currents rush
and swell the cold surrounding trunks torn
from the shore, sinking trash snagged
and flapping from branch ends, fishing line
snarled and webbed. Further, deeper, down,
bottles, cans, tires, anchors, shoes,
a cooler, and underneath, the treasures
lost: keys, an earring, sunglasses, a knife,
the daylight glint dulled, the edges mossy,
hinges dark. And on down prowl the salvage
beasts: turtle, carp, eel, mollusk
locked tight; mute sovereigns dark,
instinctive in their empire, brute mind
driving them deepest, shadowed from
the strafing sun that burns the clouds,
steams the joints of planked and sagging docks,
the bleached bows of boats straining
at their stays, singes pale shoulders
of children rushing from their porches, crashing
through the water keeping their knees
and feet twisting high, daring each
to dive, lungs tight as a dam,
eyes blinded, hands grasping, wild
to touch the terrible, shifting lakebottom.

III. Damp

Four days of rain and now the wet
has got inside the cabin, into
the foodstuffs and linens soft
and still in the kitchen; into
the shirts and shorts folded
in their dark drawer; into
the bright pages of the celebrity
magazine curling on the table,
into each playing card laid out
for solitaire; into my notebook,
unhinging the sheaf of paper
pressed into the spine;
into the blankets and quilts
twisted at the center of our bed;
and now into even the joists
and the seams of the walls,
making them sigh and swell
against each jammed door,
each buckled window frame,
sheeting again with the wake
of rain coming down
so surely I could cry.

Further Affections

While mid the busy stir and strife
Of industry the shepherd still
Enjoys his summer dreams at will

— John Clare, "July"
The Shepherd's Calendar

Shame, your seventh-grade son says;
shame, your mid-life crisis car,
your trying-to-be-cool car, your present
to yourself when you hit the curve
at forty, threatened to spin out and instead
chose this adjustment. Let him squirm
and smirk, sink into his seat as he fumbles
with his phone: some girl, a hang-up, different
ride home from the dance. Let him reach
for the dash, snarl *this music sucks.* Just smile,
then re-adjust the dial, play it all the louder.
You want to say: *It's a free country;* or
I know you are, but what am I? or, *Since
when was a convertible a crime?* But keep
it to yourself, that past July of sun and speed,
that slope of road to everywhere: the lake,
the fields, the summer breeze and her,
lips ripe and sweet as blackberries.
Let him think you are a dope, a loser,
hapless dad in a ridiculous ride, good only
for a lift, some cash. His time will come,
of party lights bright as Venus, Mars,
shining in the wide night sky, and all of it
in his orbit, shameless, poised: whole
worlds waiting his further affections.

Vacation Rental

When the sun stoops to meet the western sky
And noons hot hours have wanderd weary bye
                              —John Clare, "August"
                              The Shepherd's Calendar

You've come here for relief, but instead
bear heat that flattens the sea, a white sun
that blanches the August sky. At the shore,
a shimmer and warp above the sand hangs
where bathers stand, shifting ice chests
at their hips, singed feet spastic
to the surf. Afternoons endured
because you've paid for this escape,
a one week's lease on domestic paradise.
You *will* relax, have fun, get to know each other,
finally. But when the household explodes
this last night - close quarters, demands on money,
too much drink - and dissolution looms
as one child cries then confers in gulping whispers
to the other, when wife demanding rationales,
falls dumb, can only shrug and sway against
your rant for order among wet towels, empty cans,
magazines strewn and crumpled on the carpet,
you're the one who has to go. You get back
on the road, still holding day's long burn,
prepare to drive and drive. The low-slung moon
will scourge your midnight path inland, north.
And you feel grief like a fever breaking,
cool day rising on Catskill green.

All I Know About Love

Let's take off those pants and get into the box of reptiles!
—Host Joe Rogan
"Fear Factor: All Female Version"

And it must start, somehow
with reptiles. And women
wearing pansy-colored
halter tops, taking off
their pants and squealing,
whether with delight
or fear the casual viewer
cannot tell, but must
himself decide which babe
can earn the most points,
by retrieving the most
gold coins from the bottom
of the reptile box.

Son, a good woman will
not take off her pants
because you ask, will not
auction her shame
for shiny objects,
will not bite
the first sweet fruit
you dangle at her lips.

And though I cannot
save you from
the angle of hips
slipping forward,
the slope of a shoulder
under moonlight,
a tangle of hair
spooling like silk
through your hands,

all I know about love
does not contain
a reptile box, race
toward reward, points
awarded the last one standing.

And what slight difference
you will someday divine
between fear and delight,
hold tight when the world
cracks open, shows its black box
of desire, its treasure
of petal, earth, bright fang.

for JME

Sidelined, Coach

Boys glad at heart to play return
The shepherds to their peace sojourn
                    —John Clare, "September"
                    The Shepherd's Calendar

You tell them to *run;*
you tell them to
pass the ball;
you bark instructions,
encouragement to these little,
huffing men, spastic engines
of fist and knee,
while you sit, sidelined
with a busted ankle,
lean on the slim rail
of a metal crutch, unable
to venture even
pillowed pressure without
a shock of wheeling pain.
And still the greater ache
to sprint and kick and crash
the goal triumphant
with your team,
burns inside in your gut,
makes you furious
at the body's fragile gearworks,
how ligaments, muscles, tendons
split and rip with one misstep,
purple the entire leg, repair
a dream for spring. So sidelined

here you run the clock.
No old man at twenty-three,
these fields, this school, this job,
this temporary hobble, cane
not even fair as foreshadow
of some final whistle,
some sunset to a season
in the sky. This is still
September, the sun
burns high and hot,
the unrepentant earth
still braces for your step,
just take it now,
this lofted shot,
perfect, arc'd for you.

Driving Your Car

I sit higher,
hands wider
gripping the bony wheel.
I am at liberty,
in charge, work
the gear shaft hard
through acceleration,
brake, and with reckless
disregard for the aging
clutch, the whining pads.

I make this carriage
mine; change the settings,
the seat's recline,
the mirror's view
to rear and side, ignore
your pre-sets, change
them too. Amused, I
play the music loud,
windows down, rest
my arm to test
the weather, wind.
Leave my scent,
my skin, all evidence
of inhabitance
for your distraction
or affection. Then

braced against spent
and unforgiving shocks,
remember how you feel
the centripetal press
of every sharp curve,
the shudder and knock
of every hidden rut,
the damage done
by negligence,
on every road I drive.

Planting Dahlias with a Pick-Ax

I have made their grave:

hacked at the ground with a pick-ax
a rough plot, some inches deep,
and shoved the squat butts
to the dirt. It was a quick job
at afternoon's fade, and without
apology to the chopped roots
split white and topside,
the infant border vine slapped
by the backswing, or the brute implement
itself, blade messed with green, stuck
with grass like hair to the bone.
I rake cover with my hands,
scuff back the dry moss, wish
the best for their vegetable souls –
full sun, steady rain, mild nights –
and assume the worst. Then turn,
shave the earth under my pink nails
and let the postman now striding near
bring whatever benediction he can.

For You, October's Boy

And now and then a solitary boy
Journeying and muttering o'er his dreams of joy
                    —*John Clare*, "October"
                    The Shepherd's Calendar

All the late dahlias lighting the yard,
and the round-hipped roses, fragrant and dark;
the flash of chrysanthemums in every pot;
vegetable gardens, still green and stalked.

A startled deer across the path; a rush
of ground pheasants by your footfall flushed;
sweep of owls' wings; the calling nightingale;
Libra weighing the moon in her star-tipped scales.

And for you too, morning's witness:
first cry of light igniting white fields,
tufted fog spilling into furrows and ditches;
the ascendant sun, the imminent blue; and see,
the woman you love stepping forward,
impossible harvest balanced at her hip.

I Gave My Love A Cell Phone;
or, Technology Won't Help You Now

I gave my love a cell phone,
that had no charge to roam,
that has minutes she may measure
at ten per day, including long distance,
including text messages, including
the calls she makes that are not to me,
but connect her at innumerable points
to wider irrelevancies, greater dispersions
of her already fragmented day, her
already scattered time, which she swears
she has not enough of, but which she swears
will be healed, patched into coherence
by this cell phone, and its promise
of carpools that run tighter than a Tokyo train,
of errand-running efficiency of such bloodless
magnificence that even the dictators of small countries
will marvel; of umbilical connection to her children
who are slowly spinning out of orbit, gently
floating beyond the great moon of her influence
until we are all wireless now, the fine silver tether
of our love unspooling past the stars and comets
and the planets hugging their satellite children
tighter and tighter, from day to night to day.

Children, Sex

Even on Saturday, they cannot wait
to creep down from sleep, little heels
hard on the floor above, an avalanche
on the stairs, flat palms on our door:
What's going on in there? We scramble for robes
blankets, twist to the floor, stagger past
each other: *Can we have waffles?*

Later, assigned to other families, organized
sports, finally an empty house, a glass of wine,
and here come the neighbor boys banging,
their boards and sticks and wheels clattering
at the front door and then the back, and then:
But both of their cars are here! And as I press
myself up from your chest, I want to scream:

We have no children! We sold them to the gypsies!
but I am carried away by the thought
of a gypsy lover, wild and dark, and my hands
are quick back into your gypsy curls,
dark and wild. Now late at night,
lights low, thick quilts a tent in our bed,
the hall phone sounds its scolding alarm.

There is homework, a test, a project
to be confirmed: *Can I talk to him please?*
Wrought things, offspring. Creaturely
hazards of our desire, our own fond wish
to be immortal. Who knows their pirate souls,
the demands in their confederate hearts:
No more children. Only us. Now.

Children Will Drive You

Then there was the week we decided
to give up drinking. "Too much, too
often," we said. "And besides, what

must the boys think? Us coming through
the door each night, collapsing like sacks
of spilt grain, popping open one,

two bottles of red, surely we must
sometimes stagger, slur, exaggerate." And so
we called it quits. Took up board games,

homework help, reading the paper aloud.
And it was swell, for a while. We avoided
politics, made a calendar, took turns

cleaning up, and actually, you know,
"got ahead." But eventually everyone
got restless, shaky. The older boy

with his nervous hands, flapping
and twisting in the calm. The younger boy
returning to his quilted fortress each night,

wild stories splayed in shadows
on the wall. And us a couple of docents
in our own home, modest, deferential,

startled by the bright kitchen, the wide stairs,
the cool plane of our bed. Pretty soon,
you know, they were asking us didn't we

want a glass of wine? Offering to cork
and spill the oblation into squat goblets
set before us now, their eyes and mouths

sober slits, hands steady as they pour,
small voices as one commanding us
to now, take the brimming cup from them.

No Bigger Than a Minute

They skip unperceived into hours,
the end of the day, the week,

and before we can say the words, it is next
summer, first frost, the New Year. *Where*

did the time go? We wonder if
we might find it by calling out,

coaxing it from behind
the big couch or under the quilt,

as when a small child steps forward,
shy and new, eager to be useful.

My lost minute, we exclaim.
My nearest one come back at last.

And we hold her close again,
though she dreams of next week, next year,

the long, surging forever without us.

Advice to the Poet

after Yeats' "Adam's Curse"

Brooding, brooding Yeats, you dolt!
You missed your chance again, and no
the answer still is not "the pilgrim soul."
She has turned to you tonight and though
she says they do not talk of it at school,
it's all we have, the currency of youth
exchanged beneath the hollow moon.
And you didn't take the bait, you fool!
Now the night is dark and mild again,
and you are brooding on the old high ways of then.
Next time, try: *Your eyes, the faery light ignites*
my soul. Your lips, the blooming rose invites
my kiss. Your arms, your hair, your face, the word
you might have said, the love she might have heard.

The November Shakes

He wishes in his heart 'twas summer time again

And oft he'll clamber up a sweeing tree
To see the scarlet hunter hurry bye
And feign woud in their merry uproar be
But sullen labour hath its tethering tye
                      —*John Clare*, "November"
                            The Shepherd's Calendar

You're a man who needs a drink.

Despite all: gutters scraped, gables
painted, wife and furnace winterized,
garden rot furrowed, tilled and still
you've got November shakes. Shudder
in your gut with every paper's flutter:
end of year assessments, property accounting,
piling of receipts, evidence the year
got spent. Then more: assault
of invitations, celebrations thick
with sugared kin, packages to sort
and send, and all of it falling faster
than you could ever rake and burn.

Mornings dark, afternoons dark, midday
gray and flat, low-ceiling'd winter
bearing like a crucifix upon your back.
The strategies for breaking free all
involve complex symmetries
of overtime and mortgage, in-laws,
meals aligned along a grinding
wheel of regret and obligation.

Better take that whiskey now,

that surfaceless silk amnesiac
that stills this anxious palsy.
Like a woman's breath, warm
against your face, hear her words,
the benediction: *There's something
in the mail. Take it like a man.*

On Presuming Mr. James Caan Would Not, Under Any Circumstances, Pretzel

Is to presume wrong. Not that I would
know, really, his secret dancing heart,
or the slope of his soul under

the uber-cool Vegas veneer,
or how and why any man becomes
an actor, of his own life or another,

playing at the roles he's dealt, no
aces, nothing wild, just the usual
scrambling along for style, the witless

amble toward another wrap, the head feint
with the tailored jacket, the right shades,
and always, *always,* waiting with

an open hand for that last pass,
that final swing, that dizzy turn,
just exactly, *exactly,* what a girl wants.

Snow Day

And some to view the winter weathers
Climb up the window seat wi glee
Likening the snow to falling feathers
In fancys infant extacy
Laughing wi superstitious love
O'er visions wild that youth supplyes

— *John Clare*, "December"
The Shepherd's Calendar

Lovely the snow as it floats from the sky, and lovely
the bare trees pillowed in white; lovely the martin
tracking across the playground walk. And lovely
the shout of *Snow!* that startles the class from
its drill and practice, the lovely disorder of books
and pencils, upturned desks. *Snow.* The whispered
awe fogs the panes. *Snow.* The mathematics,
capitals a distant task. And lovely her face
when she calls dismissal, closes the ledger, abandons
the rule, follows you into the cold. She forms
a snowball with her mittened hands, tosses it wide
of the mark, and laughs.
                    Lovely then as lovely
now, knocking your boots against the step,
shaking your coat of December flurries, you
remember the arc of that toss, the snowball dark
against the spiraling sky, the dizzy horizon
receding, then near as you whirled your way out
of boyhood, walked home on your own down dusted
streets, past silent park and bridge, dreamed next
day's sleep, postponed reports, cancelled test,
and now the world grown yours to turn. Lovely
you think, the barren trees, the winter bird;
lovely, you sigh, as she welcomes you into the warm.

About the author

Lynnell Edwards is the author of *The Farmer's Daughter*, a volume of poetry published in 2003 by Red Hen Press. Her work has also appeared in *Poets Against the War*, *Oregon Poets Against the War*, and literary journals, including *Poetry East*, *Smartish Pace*, *Poems & Plays*, *The Los Angeles Review*, and others. She is also the author of a stage adaptation of *The Yellow Wallpaper*, produced in 2004 by Concordia University, and is a regular reviewer for *Pleiades*, *Rain Taxi*, and *The Georgia Review*. She is the recipient of a 2007 Al Smith Fellowship from the Kentucky Arts Council. She lives in Louisville, Kentucky.

Joel D. Levinson received a BA in Communications and Masters in Visual Arts from
The University of California, Berkeley where he received the *Eisner Award* for *Outstanding
Achievement in Photography*. As an Artist and Photographer, Levinson has had more than
thirty One-Man Museum and Gallery Exhibitions throughout North America and Europe, including:

Art Museum of South Texas-Corpus Christe, *Center for Creative Photography*-Tucson,
J.B. Speed Art Museum-Louisville, *Milwaukee Art Museum, Musee Nicephore Niepce*-France,
Sprengel Art Museum-Germany, *Wilhelm Hack Art Museum*-Germany.

Levinson has had two published books, FLEAMARKETS, and Joel D. Levinson - Photographs
And has been included in every edition of Who's Who in American Art, 1984 - 2006
There have been more than fifty Magazine and International Print Articles featuring his work including:

Art-Germany, *Artforum, Artfactum*-Belgium, *Arts, Artweek, High Performance, Horizon, Interview,
New Art International*-France, *People, Picture, Photo Communique*-Canada, *Sabado*-Mexico,

More of Joel D. Levinson's work may be viewed at: WWW.JoelDLevinson.Com